CONOZCO LAS FORMAS
I KNOW SHAPES

By Jon Welzen
Traducido por Fátima Rateb

Gareth Stevens
PUBLISHING

conceptos
básicos

¡Conozco las formas!

I know shapes!

Veo un círculo.

I see a circle.

4

5

Veo un cuadrado.

I see a square.

7

Veo un rectángulo.

I see a rectangle.

Veo un triángulo.

I see a triangle.

11

Veo una estrella.

I see a star.

Veo un rombo.

I see a diamond.

15

Veo un óvalo.

I see an oval.

17

Veo un octágono.

- -

I see an octagon.

¡Veo círculos
en un rectángulo!

I see circles
in a rectangle!

21

¿Qué formas ves?

What shapes
do you see?

23

Please visit our website, www.garethstevens.com. For a free color catalog of all our high-quality books, call toll free 1-800-542-2595 or fax 1-877-542-2596.

Cataloging-in-Publication Data

Names: Welzen, Jon.
Title: I know shapes = Conozco las formas / Jon Welzen.
Description: New York : Gareth Stevens Publishing, 2017. | Series: What I know = Lo que conozco | In English and Spanish
Identifiers: ISBN 9781482462050 (library bound)
Subjects: LCSH: Geometry–Juvenile literature.
Classification: LCC QA445.5 W45 2017 | DDC 516'.15–dc23

First Edition

Published in 2017 by
Gareth Stevens Publishing
111 East 14th Street, Suite 349
New York, NY 10003

Copyright © 2017 Gareth Stevens Publishing

Translator: Fátima Rateb
Editorial Director, Spanish: Nathalie Beullens-Maoui
Editor, English: Therese Shea
Designer: Sarah Liddell

Photo credits: Cover, p. 1 (stripes) Eky Studio/Shutterstock.com; cover, p. 1 (blocks) Smolina Marianna/Shutterstock.com; p. 3 AlyssaV/Shutterstock.com; p. 5 rangizzz/Shutterstock.com; p. 7 endeavor/Shutterstock.com; p. 9 jakkapan/Shutterstock.com; p. 11 Mau Horng/Shutterstock.com; p. 13 Jorg Hackemann/Shutterstock.com; p. 15 Earl D. Walker/Shutterstock.com; p. 17 Coprid/Shutterstock.com; p. 19 Peter Gudella/Shutterstock.com; p. 21 Africa Studio/Shutterstock.com; p. 23 Petr Novotny/Shutterstock.com.

Printed in the United States of America

CPSIA compliance information: Batch #CW17GS: For further information contact Gareth Stevens, New York, New York at 1-800-542-2595.